Tell Me Your Story

Tell Me Your Story

Jane D. Kelly

iUniverse, Inc.
New York Lincoln Shanghai

Tell Me Your Story

iUniverse books may be ordered through booksellers or by contacting:

iUniverse
2021 Pine Lake Road, Suite 100
Lincoln, NE 68512
www.iuniverse.com
1-800-Authors (1-800-288-4677)

Because of the dynamic nature of the Internet, any Web addresses or links contained in this book may have changed since publication and may no longer be valid.

The views expressed in this work are solely those of the author and do not necessarily reflect the views of the publisher, and the publisher hereby disclaims any responsibility for them.

ISBN: 978-0-595-45047-3 (pbk)
ISBN: 978-0-595-89358-4 (ebk)

Printed in the United States of America

Contents

PART I
History of Plowshares

1

An Invitation

Little did I dream that an invitation from Martin Bradley on an August morning in 1983 would change my life forever!

I was sitting at the desk in my office when I felt a presence at the open door. I looked up to find Martin standing in the doorway.

"Sister Jane, would you have time to talk to me?" he asked. Promptly replied, "Of course, Martin, come in and have a seat."

Having settled in his chair, he asked, "How would you like to open a Community Dining Room to feed the poor and homeless in Ukiah, Sister?"

"Martin, I have dreamed of that for years. Nothing would give me more pleasure."

"Sister Jane, a local church opened a soup kitchen and insisted that the guests listen to Bible readings as they ate which meant that they could not talk. As a result the numbers dropped till none were showing up and they closed the program."

"Martin, we need to formulate our policies regarding our program before we do anything else. If you have the time, I think we should do it now."

"Sister, I have the time."

We began to brainstorm what our policies would be.

First of all, we would follow Father Alfred Boeddeker's policy when he opened Saint Anthony's Dining Room in San Francisco which serves 2,000 people a day. They would be welcomed as he would welcome a guest in his own house. They would be treated with dignity and not be held hostage to listening to Bible readings.

"Secondly, we would not ask questions of our guests and would welcome all who came to our door as long as they are not under the influence of drugs or alcohol."

"It would be a family dining room where parents felt safe enough to bring their children for a meal."

Lastly, what should we name the building?

After some thought, I suggested to Martin, "Let's take the name from Isaiah 2: 4[1], which reads, "They shall beat their swords into plowshares."

Our goal was not to just offer a meal but also to inform people as to why there was hunger in the world.

We decided on "Plowshares Community Dining Room and Peace and Justice Center."

Martin would put out a monthly newsletter, the Advocate, that would deal with peace and justice issues in the world and solicit funds for the project. The Advocate would also share stories about the operations and the guests who came to the Dining Room.

In parting, I said to Martin, "You find the building and I'll find the money."

After Martin left I asked myself, "Where in the world, Jane, are you going to find the money?"

I remembered that the pastors in the local parishes met once a month as a Ministerial Association. What better source for asking financial help for our program!

That afternoon, I called one of the pastors and asked if I could be put on the agenda for the next meeting.

I was granted my request.

At the meeting, I pointed out that the churches were giving out food vouchers costing $4.95 to the poor who came to their door. When Plowshares opens its door, they could tell the individuals asking for vouchers to go to Plowshares for a meal.

My request was to donate $100.00 a month to support Plowshares.

Three pastors agreed to donate $100.00 a month. Joseph Crowell, who was in charge of Saint Mary's Saint Vincent DePaul Society, pledged $300.00 a month. I knew we had enough money to pay the rent.

The pastor of the Nazarene Church said, "Sister, we are a small congregation so we can't pledge money but we can lend you our tables and chairs for the Dining Room."

As I was leaving, the Methodist pastor caught up with me and pointed out that we would need seed money. He said he would advance two years of their pledge, which came to $2400.00!

We had the money to get us started!

---

1.   The New American Bible, Thomas Nelson Publishers New York, 1970. Pg.779.

2

Securing the Money and the Building

I called Martin and informed him of the good news that some of the churches agreed to pledge us $100.00 a month and the Methodist church advanced us $2400.00.

Then Martin shared his good news.

"Sister Jane, I met with Francine Long, the realtor for Dr. Trucker, a plastic surgeon in Santa Rosa who owned the old Social Services buildings on Main Street and was willing to rent the buildings for $300.00 a month until he sells them. I have set a meeting date with a group of people who are interested in helping us."

The following week we met in a dark, cold room in the main building on Main Street since the electricity was not turned on. The purpose of the meeting was to assign areas of responsibility.

The job of renovating the building would be Martin's responsibility.

Sister Jane would be in charge of financing and soliciting volunteers to cook and serve the meal as well as cleanup. She would approach the Episcopal Church to take Thursday as their day to cook using their kitchen. Saint Mary of the Angels would be asked to take Tuesday and use Saint Mary's School kitchen.

Ginny Lindstead would organize the Methodist Church and use their church hall kitchen.

Ginny turned to me and asked, "Sister Jane, will you be involved for a few years?" My response was, "Ginny, I will be involved until they carry me out in a body bag!"

With that, she handed me a check for $300.00.

Debra Meek, Susan Crane, Mary Rice and Heidi Vaughan would purchase the necessary equipment for the Dining Room and would explore the means to acquire food for the daily meal.

Debra would also be responsible for Mondays and arrange to use the Saturday Afternoon Club's kitchen.

Martin had a crew renovating the building the very next weekend. It was a challenge since the building we would use for the dining room had small cubicles that had served as offices for the social workers. These all had to be removed. The other building was to be used for storage.

It was decided that Martin would be the director, and he agreed to withhold his salary until we had sufficient funds to pay him.

Our first Advocate came out in September, 1983 and it was mailed to people whom we felt would donate.

Later, when we opened our doors, the Ukiah Daily Journal sent Faye Woodward to cover the story. She had pictures taken and wrote a marvelous feature article on our Dining Room. She later followed it up with other feature articles.

We had a family of eight, the Graves who came daily to the Dining Room and Faye featured them in an article with pictures.

Because of these articles, our donor base increased.

Our next challenge was to find the food we would need for the meals.

Debra, Susan, Mary Rice and Heidi approached local stores requesting groceries that they would otherwise discard, and agreed to pick them up each morning.

Thanks to Governor Jerry Brown who made it legal for stores to give their surplus food to non-profit organizations, stores were willing to give us their surplus food.

In the beginning we received some produce that was not edible; but as time went by and we got to know the managers of produce, we would get crates of produce that had not even been opened.

Martin arranged for us to receive government surplus commodities which included cheese, canned pork, pasta, butter, canned fruit, rice, peanut butter and more.

Martin went out to the local stores who had agreed to give us produce and other food that they would otherwise discard, and collected what we would need to prepare the meal for the next day. He did this each day until we had money to hire someone to do the daily run.

Another source of food came from the game warden who would bring us animals that had been illegally shot. Our first animal was a bear and thankfully we had a butcher in Potter Valley who agreed to package the meat for us. We rented a freezer to store it. Among the animals that we received were deer, pigs and at one time, pounds of abalone.

One day George Sullivan thawed out roasts and when it came time to serve them, he donned a tall white chef's hat and white jacket and as the guests came through the line, he would ask, "Do you want rare, medium-rare or well-done?" A mother and her little daughter came to be served and the mother pointed to the meat and said to her daughter, "Honey, this is a roast."

I had to fight back tears realizing that the child had never seen a roast.

On another occasion, I came to the dining room and noticed a family of four waiting to go in. I had to run an errand and when I came back I noticed that the father and boy were still sitting on the bench.

"Sister, we have only two pairs of shoes and you have to wear shoes in the Dining Room so I had my wife and daughter go in first."

"Sir, what sizes are your shoes?" I asked him.

Armed with this information, I dashed over to the Dorcas Society which gives out free clothes and shoes. Thankfully they were open. I went in and picked up four pairs of shoes and socks and hurried back to the Dining Room and gave them to the father and said, "Now you can join your wife and daughter for the meal." Again, I had to fight back the tears to think that they didn't have shoes!

I recall people telling me when it was known that we were opening a Dining Room for the poor and homeless, "Sister, we don't have poor and homeless people in Ukiah." My reply was, "Great! We'll open the doors and no one will come."

That myth was dispelled when we served forty people the day we opened our doors. Daily the number increased to a point that at times we were serving over one hundred people.

I remember one day a gentleman drove up with a trunk full of cheese and informed us that he had to discard it because the date for selling it had expired. He went on to say, "My mother would kill me if she found out that I had thrown it away!" Thank God for his mother!

Soon local bakeries donated their day-old bread and pastries.

Because of the donations we were able to serve a salad, main dish, fresh vegetables, bread and butter and a dessert. Often we would have a fruit salad.

Milk, orange juice and coffee were served.

I maintained that we had the best restaurant in town. The food was excellent, the price was right and you didn't need a reservation!

In the beginning we used paper plates and plastic silverware until we had enough money to purchase plastic trays, silverware and mugs.

3

The Door is Open

On November 14, 1983, we opened our doors and served the first meal.

Our policy was that we would not serve anyone who was under the influence of drugs or alcohol because it was a family restaurant.

I remember one day two men were holding up their friend who was obviously under the influence of alcohol and approached the door to the dining room. They said, "Sister, our friend didn't sleep well last night so he is very sleepy and we are holding him up lest he fall.

I informed them that their friend because he was obviously under the influence of alcohol could not come in. "When your friend is sober we will serve him a meal." The next day he returned sober and never again came when he was drinking.

In all of the years that we have been open, only a handful have been turned away because they were under the influence of drugs or alcohol!

Word travels fast among the homeless.

The cooks not only prepared and cooked the meal they had to clean up as well. We were afraid that they would burnout so we contracted with UVA (Ukiah Valley Association for Habilitation) to clean up after the cooks and set up the dining room for the next day's meal.

Jan Hildebrand was the supervisor whom they sent along with Randy, Gary, Jane and Connie to fulfill the contract. They proved to be a godsend for the cooks!

When you serve homeless people you come to realize that they have other needs apart from a meal. Among those needs are gas to get to the Dining Room, diapers for their babies, money for prescription drugs and medical attention.

Martin and I began to respond to their needs even to the point of paying for gas, medicine and diapers.

It became overwhelming. I remember the afternoon when all the guests and helpers left; we sat down as we did each day and evaluated the day's operation. At one point we burst into tears and acknowledged that we couldn't keep up with all the needs of the homeless. In that moment we said, "All we can do is feed the poor and the homeless and forego trying to respond to all their other needs."

We have kept to that decision and it has cut our stress level down considerably. Another decision we made was that we would not lend or give money to those who asked. It is also a policy that we have kept.

There were times when we praised ourselves, for example, the time when Diana came to us pregnant with her first child. She had been addicted to drugs, and when she found out that she was pregnant she checked herself into the Ford Street Project to get the help she needed to stop taking drugs. At the time she was homeless and Ford Street, when she stopped taking drugs, put her into transitional housing. We would give her food for the weekend and milk as well. Diana would come to the dining room each day, help out and get her hot, nutritious meal which certainly benefited the baby. She gave birth to a healthy baby girl named Regina. Diana would bring her to Plowshares and proudly show her to the volunteers before she ate her meal. Regina came to be known as "the Plowshares Baby."

I longed for the day that we would have our own kitchen where we wouldn't have to rely on kitchens apart from the Dining Room to prepare and cook our meals. Each day we would have to bring the food and condiments to the kitchen for that day's meal.

4

Eviction

The dreaded day that Dr. Trucker sold the buildings finally dawned. We were evicted in June and ended up serving the meals in the park.

Martin arranged with the city that we could serve our guests in the park, but for only two weeks! It meant that each day Martin would transport the tables and chairs to the park on Dora Street. They were stored in his pickup truck.

When the two weeks were up, we moved to Saint Mary of the Angels' parking lot. Thankfully it had a small building that boasted a bathroom and running water and electrical outlets, as well as a room large enough to store our tables and chairs. We were able to make the coffee there and had storage space for both coffee and paper goods.

Martin and I walked the streets of Ukiah looking for a building. Each day after the meal was served and the clean-up completed, we would set off with the listings that we received from the realtors of vacant buildings.

We discovered a building on Cherry Street that was once a shirt factory. Martin found the owner and we drew up a contract that met with the owner's approval. Since the building was also owned by another partner, it had to be approved by him. Unfortunately he informed us that he had other plans for the building and couldn't rent it to us.

The building is still vacant. I believe that he didn't want it to be used as a Dining Room for the poor and the homeless.

Once again with listings in hand we set out again in our quest for a building. It was August and the temperatures rose to 120 degrees on some days. It was on such a day that I told Martin, "I can't go on. It's too hot!"

Thank God I agreed to go one more block which brought us to Luce Avenue just off State Street. Eureka! We looked up the block and there was a church building for lease! Having arrived at the building, we began to look through the windows. I cried out, "Martin, it has a kitchen. We have found our building!"

Martin looked up the owner's name and gave me his name and phone number.

It was Sunday morning and I called the owner about leasing the building. He told me, "Sister, a man in the Bay Area told me that he would call me by 2:00 p.m. today and let me know if he decided to rent the building. If he doesn't call, you can lease the building." How I prayed! One minute after 2:00 p.m., I called and was greatly relieved when the landlord said, "Sister, the gentleman did not call so you can lease the building for $300.00 a month."

"I'll bring the money to you now," I assured him.

"Sister, that won't be necessary. You can bring the money tomorrow and I will draw up the lease and you can pay me then," he told me.

As soon as I hung up, I called Martin and said, "Martin, we have the building. We are to bring a check for $300.00 and sign the lease." It was arranged that we would go the next day at 10:00 a.m. With check in hand, Martin and I met with the owner and signed the lease. We left with the keys to our new location! We were ecstatic with joy! We now had a Dining Room with a kitchen!

5

Our New Building

With a great deal of enthusiasm, Martin got a crew together and on the first weekend renovated the interior of the building to make it ready to serve our first meal on the following Monday.

A wall was removed so as to make more space for the dining area.

There was another room off of the kitchen where we had a counter built to sort out the food that was collected from the stores. Martin, with the help of a carpenter, installed a door so that the truck could pull up and get the commodities unloaded. It also gave us space for our two small freezers and our commercial dishwasher.

Given the amount of perishable food that was collected each day, the commercial refrigerator could not hold it all. We needed a walk-in refrigerator.

To pay for a walk-in, I wrote a hundred people from our donor list and asked if they would loan us a hundred dollars and we would repay it on a first come basis. Within a week we had the money!

I noticed that a lady whose address was listed at a senior mobile park on Gobbi Street had sent us a check for seven hundred fifty dollars, and I was concerned that she could not be able to afford it. I called her to tell her of my concern.

She laughed and said, "Sister, my husband and I were in the restaurant business for years and we know you can't run a restaurant without a walk-in refrigerator. Yes, we can afford it, and thank you for your concern."

It soon became obvious that we needed a walk-in freezer to store the turkeys that we received at Thanksgiving and the hams at Christmas as well as the frozen meat that people donated when they emptied their freezers. It would be the meat that would last us through the year.

So once again, I wrote a letter requesting a loan for a walk-in freezer and once again we had the money within a week.

I came in on our first Monday after opening and found a yellow piece of paper with twenty numbers listed on it and a note telling me that I could list twenty items we needed for the kitchen. It was a local cabinetmaker who had left the note.

Martin and I put our heads together and came up with the twenty needs. Among them were shelves in the room adjacent to the kitchen which we had designated for storage. We listed cabinets and shelves in the kitchen to store our pots, pans and utensils and a long serving counter in the dining room where we could install the steam table and have space to lay out the salad, bread and desserts as well as space for the trays and silverware. We realized it would be more economical to buy plastic trays and silverware.

A gentleman who came to the dining room had started his own cleaning business, and in gratitude, he came and stripped the floors, washed, waxed and polished them. The floors were sparkling!

It was a jubilant day when we abandoned the parking lot and cooked our first meal and served it in the new building!

6

Ever since we first started serving meals to the homeless and we saw that the children were dirty, because there was no place that a homeless person could shower or bathe, I wanted to take them home and put them in a tub and wash them clean. You could see that their clothes had not seen a washing machine in probably weeks. There was no place to wash your clothes except at a Laundromat, and that took money that some could not afford.

I dreamed of the day that we could open a Personal Care Center where the homeless could shower and wash their clothes. You can't go for a job interview in dirty clothes!

When I heard that a homeless woman was fired because she would go in early and shower at the convalescent home where she worked, I was determined to find a building where we could open a Personal Care Center.

One Thanksgiving in 1992 a reporter from the Ukiah Daily Journal appeared in the kitchen and asked if he could interview the cooks regarding what they would like to see happen this Thanksgiving. I said," Yes, provided I could express my wish first."

"And what would that be, Sister?" he asked.

"I would like to open a Personal Care Center where homeless people could shower and wash their clothes." The request was printed in the paper. Later I received a call from Diane, our director, who said that someone had sent a check for a Personal Care Center. I thought to myself, "It probably is ten or twenty dollars."

I asked her, "How much is it, Diane?"

She said, "Sister, it is a check for four thousand dollars."

I knew then that this was a mandate to open a Personal Care Center.

Once again I took to the streets with a listing of buildings that were for rent in hopes of finding a suitable building for the center. My quest was in vain. There was just one house that I thought could be suitable but it had already been rented.

That night, I sat up straight in bed and said to myself, "Build it at Plowshares!" "That way we wouldn't have to look over two sites," I told myself.

The very next morning, I called Fontaine McFadden, who I knew had money, in hopes that she would help.

"Fontaine, I want to add a wing onto Plowshares for a Personal Care Center. Could you help me?" I asked.

"Sister, I'm meeting with my contractor and electrician right now. We will meet you at Plowshares shortly."

When they arrived, I showed them where I thought we could build the addition. I pointed out the west side of the building and the electrician said after walking around the building it should be added on the east side since that was where the electrical boxes were located.

Having thanked them, I began to plan what my next move should be in building the annex. It soon came when I was at a meeting with City Planners and I told them of my plan to build a Personal Care Center for the homeless.

I no sooner expressed my desire than a card was passed along to me.

It was a business card from Robert Clark that indicated he was a contractor.

On the back of the card he wrote, "Sister, see me after the meeting."

I waited for him after the meeting and introduced myself.

"I know who you are, Sister, as does most everyone in the community."

He went on to say, "Every year North Coast Builders takes on a project cost-free. We will take on your project this year."

I had a sudden urge to embrace him, which I did, and thanked him profusely!

We set a date to meet at Plowshares the next day at 10:00 a.m.

10:00 a.m. came and so did Robert!

I pointed out where we intended to add the new part of the building. He approved of the location.

I asked him, "Could you give me a ballpark figure as to what it will cost to build the annex?"

"Sister, I think it will cost about $20,000.00 since I know that I can get building materials donated as well as volunteer laborers."

Even so where was I going to get that amount of money?

Our landlord gave the approval for the addition and offered to lend us the money. However, I didn't want to pay interest on a loan so I thanked him and looked elsewhere for the funds.

"Where was elsewhere?" I asked myself.

I wrote a letter to my Congregation and asked for the funds. Within a week, I received a check for $20,000.00!

We hired Bob Axt to be our architect and he did a wonderful job of utilizing every inch of space so that we could install four showers and a disabled access bathroom that had a sink and counter where parents could bathe their infants.

I insisted that the showers should be tiled and the waiting room with the cabinets to be done in wood grain. I didn't want the facility to look like a gym but like a room you would find in an upscale hotel.

Having the necessary funds to begin construction, we needed to get a use permit from the City Planning Commission. We were placed on the agenda and made our proposal to build an annex to Plowshares' building on Luce Avenue. The night that the Commission would consider our proposal it was decided that I would do the talking. When I spoke to our proposal, the Chairman of the Commission kept suggesting other sites, that he thought would be more suitable. I explained to him that the sites he suggested were too distant for the homeless. Building the Center at Plowshares would mean that the homeless could receive all of our services at one location. The Commissioners took a break and when they came back I was dumbfounded to hear the Chairman make a motion to approve the use permit for the Personal Care Center to be open from 7:00 a.m. to 9:00 p.m. seven days a week!

I contacted Robert Clark and asked, "How soon can you start the construction?" "We can begin next week," he told me.

On Monday the first heavy piece of equipment arrived that would be used to dig the foundation.

We broke ground on October 6, 1993, just ten years after opening the Dining Room! The building was completed in January.

My next challenge was to find someone to supervise the operation of people taking showers and washing their clothes.

Carole Wells called me and said, "Sister Jane, Sister Thelma, a Franciscan Sister, is moving to Ukiah to care for her aging parents and is looking for a ministry."

"Carole, I have the perfect ministry for her," I replied. "Let me know when she arrives and I will meet with her."

On January 1st I met with Sister Thelma at the Personal Care Center and was delighted when she agreed to supervise the operation. Thelma and I spent two days sorting out the soaps, shampoos wash cloths and towels. We made available sweatsuits that could be worn while the persons were waiting for their clothes to dry.

We were ready to open our doors to the Personal Care Center!

On February 1, 1993, the Feast of the Purification, we welcomed our first guest.

Thanks to a donor, we acquired a barber chair, and someone volunteered to come daily and give haircuts.

When our guests left the Center, they were wellgroomed!

Outreach workers come once a week and do HIV testing.

For three years we had a volunteer doctor who came once a week to screen any guest who felt they had a health problem. That service is no longer necessary since a free clinic has opened in Ukiah.

Homeless people use Plowshares' address to receive mail and we installed a phone that is used for our guests to apply for jobs. They can give that number for employers and others to contact them.

We believe that we have touched all the bases regarding the needs of the homeless that we can offer. Unfortunately, housing was not one of them and that is the greatest need. They simply cannot afford what it takes to get into housing. Since you need to pay the first and last months' rent as well as a cleaning fee, their income was not sufficient to cover these costs.

In 2004 the Ford Street Project opened the Buddy Eller Center Homeless Shelter, but the problem of homelessness is still much larger than a shelter can solve.

I learned a great deal about housing when I received a grant from the Eriksen Foundation for $10,000, to help homeless people. I would pay the last months rent and the cleaning fee. They had to assure me that they could afford the monthly rent. In the three years that I received the grant money, I was able to get thirty-one families into housing.

I remember the day when I took a family to their house. The children delighted in running up and down the front steps. Their mother informed me, "Sister, they have never seen steps before!"

Our building proved adequate for our purposes but the time constraints on our meal service meant that we could only operate for one hour each day proved a challenge. I wonder how many restaurants can serve one hundred people in one hour! Our doors opened at 11:15 a.m. and closed at 12:15 p.m. We were granted only two weekends a year that we could be open. We only received this because Christmas Eve fell on a Sunday and we needed to get permission from the City Building Department to serve our Christmas meal and give out toys to the children.

Apart from having an adequate dining room and Personal Care Center, we are blessed with a marvelous staff that work so well together and treat our guests with dignity.

Mary Buckley, Executive Director and Advocate Editor, spends her time supervising the staff and writing grants which would prove so wonderful when we decided to build a new facility where we would have no time restraints.

Rhonda De Los Santos is our Operations Manager who runs the kitchen and supervises the volunteers. She does a great job.

Beverley Metcalf, who is Office Manager and works so well with Rhonda, relieves Mary of many office jobs so as to free her up for other duties.

Rhonda and Beverley or other staff greet our guests at the door each day and usher them into the Dining Room.

Pilar Moreno, Program Aide, is a great help to Rhonda.

Veronica Martinez, Personal Care Coordinator, runs a smooth operation, getting people in and out of the showers and supervises the washing and drying of their clothes.

Roy Framke, Food Share Manager, makes the daily rounds to pick up produce and food from the stores. He sorts the food and takes what is left over to the Food Bank and other agencies serving low-income people. He has been with us fourteen years and does a great job.

We looked forward to the day when we could build our own new building that would be free of time constraints.

The day dawned when we had concrete evidence that a new building was in sight.

Genevieve Curran, a sister to Sister Agnes Curran, PBVM, passed away and willed $27,000.00 to Plowshares for a new building!

I saw it as a mandate to begin a building fund for a new building.

7

A New Building

The fund began to increase. I received a half million dollars from a friend; we wrote a grant for one million dollars from the State via the City of Ukiah, and secured other grants and donations.

With Mary's fundraising and with Jack Daniels, our treasurer, investing our money wisely, we purchased a piece of property on South State Street.

We hired Bob Axt to be our architect for the new facility. He had designed the Personal Care Center and did a marvelous job.

On a hot (115 degrees) Saturday morning on July 22, 2006, we broke ground for the new building. Despite the heat, over three hundred people attended the groundbreaking celebration.

Mary prepared a moving ceremony in which representatives from several religions were asked to say a prayer and shovel out dirt.

She had each person in attendance write blessings for the new facility. These were collected and placed in a container to be buried in the hole made by the ministers. The ministers included Buddhist monks, a Catholic priest, a member of the Jewish community, a Christian minister and a Native American.

Tents, tables and chairs were set up. The Savings Bank of Mendocino paid for the chicken that was to be barbequed to feed the people. Volunteers made the salad and we purchased bread to go with the meal. Drinks were served as well as dessert. A band played music. It proved to be a great celebration!

We hope to begin construction soon with the hope of opening the doors to our new building soon in 2008.

I wrote this history hoping that it would be an incentive for people in other communities to open a building to serve the homeless in their areas.

It was through Plowshares that I was able to meet homeless people and hear their stories of how they came to be homeless.

PART II
Tell Me Your Story

8

Introduction

I followed the same approach with each individual I interviewed.

When I approached someone on the parking lot, I would ask their name and say, "Are you homeless?" If they said, "Yes.", I would explain that I am writing a book on homelessness and would they be willing to tell me their story. Much to my amazement, they were more than willing. I assured them that I would not use their full name, only their first.

These were the questions that I asked:

Where were you born?

What was your home life like?

When and why did you leave home and end up on the streets?

How did you support yourself?

These are their stories.

9

I Was Sold as a Prostitute

Cindy came to Plowshares each day for a meal and also to wash her clothes. She would often be seen in the Personal Care Center helping out. At other times you would see her in the Dining Room helping out with the meal. One day I took her aside and asked if she was homeless. Her answer was, "Sister, I have been homeless for over eight years. I live in my small used RV with my dog."

"Cindy, Where were you born?"

"I was born in Miami, Oklahoma on November 11, 1962."

I went on to ask her what her home life was like.

"When I was five years old, my mother had me dance naked in bars to make money. At the age of fifteen, she sold me as a prostitute and I went from man to man.

"Several times I tried to kill my mother by stabbing her. She never reported it because she would be found guilty of child abuse."

"Cindy, did your father ever try to intervene?"

"He left us when I was two and I never knew him."

"Later I found out that he sent letters to me but my mother never gave them to me. She burned them."

Cindy went on to tell me, "My mother did do one thing right by me and that is she insisted that I go to school. I graduated from college and secured an excellent job that paid well. I married the first man who asked me to marry him to get away from the abusive situation. My mother abused me physically and on several occasions, she would stick hair pins in my ears and as a result my hearing became impaired. I went from one abusive situation to another. Shortly after I got married, my husband would get drunk and physically abuse me. I left him." I have been married seven times and each time I was physically abused."

"One day I went to work and had a panic attack. I left the office never to return. I stayed in my apartment and only left to buy food. I panicked every time

I came in contact with a group of people." My money soon ran out and I was evicted and ended up living in my car."

"Because of my disability, I receive SSI which pays me $900.00 a month but is not enough to get into housing. I can't afford the first and last months rent plus the cleaning fee."

"I was able to buy a used R.V. and that became my home."

"Cindy, you don't seem to find it disconcerting to come to Plowshares," I said to her.

"The first time I came to Plowshares, I felt safe and comfortable and that is why I come every day. Everybody is so friendly."

"How did you come to move to Ukiah?" I asked.

One day my mother gave me a letter from my father and he was asking that I visit him in Ukiah, California."

"I came to Ukiah and met my father. It was a joyous reunion and we hugged each other and cried."

"The last time he saw me I was two years old and I, of course, didn't remember him."

"Unfortunately there is no room for me in his small apartment and he didn't have money to put me up in an apartment. He is on a very fixed income. However, he looks after me and makes sure that I am safe."

One day I noticed that Cindy was very happy and asked her, "Why do you seem so happy today?"

"Sister, my husband is in prison and I get to visit him on Saturday. I hope we have conjugal rights."

"Drugs and a gun were found in his car when he was stopped by a policeman for running a red light. He told me that the gun and drugs were left in his car by a friend."

On the following Monday, Cindy told me that they did not have conjugal rights but he was to get out of prison in eight weeks.

"Sister, I can hardly wait!" she exclaimed.

Cindy went on to tell me that her husband is a" street corner preacher" and sings and preaches to people who come up to him.

They met in Arizona and she joined him and sang along with him on the street.

When George, her husband, was arrested she moved to Ukiah to be with her father. George would join her when he was released.

I met George when he joined Cindy at the Plowshare's Volunteer Appreciation luncheon.

He was a tall, handsome black man with gracious manners.

He shared with me that he had gone back to college and hoped to get a degree in psychology. He wanted to be a psychologist and work counseling people. I could see that he would be a very good one.

I remembered that Cindy once told me that she was unable to get housing because they didn't want to rent to a mixed couple. I told her it was against the law and she should seek legal advice.

They left the luncheon hand-in-hand. They appeared to be very much in love so I was surprised when Cindy told me, "George left me for another woman. He has moved in with her. He claims that I was unfaithful when he was in prison."

"I never slept with another man while you were in prison. I was faithful!" I told him.

I hadn't seen Cindy for several weeks and was greatly relieved when she returned to Plowshares!

She had purchased a new motor home and it was so much larger than the small trailer that she was living in before. She is happy and doing very well.

10

My Father Was the Chief of Police

One day I drove into the parking lot at Plowshares and a man and woman came up to the car door. The man opened the door and the woman helped me out.

"What are your names?" I asked.

"I'm Richard and this is Betty," the man responded.

"My name is Sister Jane," I said.

"Oh, Sister we know who you are. You started Plowshares."

I asked if they were homeless and they both said they were staying at the homeless shelter.

Because they seemed so friendly, I explained to them that I was writing a book on homelessness and wondered if they would share their story with me.

They both agreed and Betty went first. "Sister, I was born in Tiffin, Ohio on November 7, 1958, and went all through Catholic schools. My father was the Chief of Police in our small town in Ohio."

"When I was six years old, my father began to sexually molest me. I went to my mother and told her what my father was doing to me. She hit me and told me not to tell lies about my father!"

"Every Sunday we would go to Mass and my father made certain that we sat in the front row where everyone could see him with his family. To me this seemed so hypocritical."

"I couldn't go to the police because my father was the Chief of Police and they would only ignore me."

"When I turned seventeen, I went to the next town and reported to the police that my father was sexually abusing me. They arrested my father and he later died in prison."

"My mother was furious because I had turned my father in and threw me out of the house! I didn't know what to do. I was so afraid that I went to the parish priest, Father Mark, and told him what had happened."

"Father Mark said that I could stay in the rectory that night and that he would work something out so that I wouldn't end up living on the street."

"The next day it was arranged that I would have dinner in the rectory and sleep there at night. During the day I went to school and after school I would go to the library until it was time for dinner."

"Sister, I was so grateful to Father Mark! He wanted to get me away from my mother so he sent me to live in a rectory in another state."

"I got an after school job at a local dry goods store and earned enough to buy a used car."

"Once again the priest sent me to another rectory in another state, and this continued until I reached California. At this time I only had a car and no job. I was told that I could no longer live in the rectory so I ended up sleeping in my car."

"I began looking for a job and finally got one working at McDonald's but it didn't pay enough to get into housing."

"A friend of mine said that she was going to Ukiah to live with a friend and invited me to go along assuring me that her friend would take me in also. We traveled to Ukiah and the friend agreed to take me in but not permanently since the apartment was small. After two weeks, I was asked to move out and I ended up in the homeless shelter."

"I was grateful to Plowshares where I could get a meal and wash my clothes."

"I finally got a job at Wal-Mart and began working overtime. I took my lunch break at the time Plowshares served its meal."

"Sister, I found an apartment on Henry Street and will be moving in on December 5th!"

"For years I could never cry regardless of how sad and frightened I was until one day the dam broke and I could no longer hold in the tears. I burst out crying and cried for hours!"

"I wrote this poem to express my feelings. Sister, this copy is for you to thank you for your love and support."

Tears

For years I knew not what a tear meant.
Thrashing tears from the depth of

Some divine despair
Rise in the heart, to the eyes.
I know what the cage bird feels.
A pain still throbs on an old scar.
I wear a mask that hides the shades
Of my eyes
Torn and bleeding in hidden grief
In shame I hide my tears
Hesitating to let one tear fall for fear my
Weakness might show
In the hollow pit of my soul deep into
The darkness
The devastation of a child's cry is silenced
By fear
Bless this day the bird flies free
The tears are broken from its cage
Cleansing the eyes from shades of
Yesterday's grief …

Betty no longer comes to Plowshares. I miss seeing her, but I'm delighted that she has finally found a home.

11

I Was in Prison for Five Years

When I arrive at Plowshares, Richard is often there to open the car door and help me out.

This morning, I asked Richard if he would share his story with me.

Richard blurted out, "Sister, I won't lie to you! I was in prison for five years."

I asked, "Could we begin at the beginning, Richard?"

"Where were you born? I was born in Alameda County, Oakland, California in 1951." Richard responded.

"Richard, I grew up in Oakland. Where did you live in Oakland?" I asked.

"We lived on 22nd Avenue just off of Fruitvale Avenue," Richard said.

"My family lived on 23rd Avenue off of Fruitvale Avenue," I informed him.

"We could have been neighbors!" I exclaimed.

"However, I moved to San Francisco before you were born."

"Richard, what was your home life like? My home life was hell, Sister."

"My Father began to sexually abuse me when I turned five years old. My mother physically abused me and did nothing to stop my father from sexually abusing me. She told me that I was lying."

"We moved from Oakland to Windsor, California when I was in high school. The abuse was getting worse at home so I moved out and lived on the streets.

"I got in with the wrong crowd and began to use drugs. I was on heroin from 1969 to 1979

"Richard, how did you support yourself?"

"I got odd jobs and I won't lie to you. Sister, I took to stealing. I was arrested for possession of drugs and sent to prison for five years. I lost my Social Security benefits and received only General Assistance which was $110.00 a month."

"I began to drink to the point that I never knew a sober day.

One day a friend invited me to go to church with him. While I was there, God came into my life and I stopped drinking. I know the man upstairs is taking care of me. I'm staying at the homeless shelter and working with a case worker. She got me on SSI and is working on getting me into housing. She handles my money and pays my bills. I receive money to pay for my needs."

"I have been clean for four months and twenty-eight days."

"Richard, are you in touch with your parents?"

"They divorced but I talk to my mother every week and I saw her on Christmas."

"Richard, you should be very proud of yourself. You have overcome huge obstacles and have come out on top!"

12

My Name Is Elizabeth

"Good morning, Virginia."

"Sister, my name is Elizabeth I was named for St. John the Baptist's mother, Elizabeth, and for the queen of England!"

"Elizabeth, I won't forget again. I'll think of the Queen of England and know that your name is Elizabeth. I'm writing a book on homelessness and wondered if you would tell me your story."

"Will my story be in your book?" she asked.

I assured her that it would be included in my book.

"I was born in Oklahoma and my parents moved to Eureka, California when I was a baby."

"I didn't have much of a childhood since my mother worked two jobs and I had to take care of my two brothers and sister. I rebelled and my mother couldn't control me, so she put me in foster care. I was a problem child so I moved from foster home to foster home. Finally my mother sent me to live with my father in Maine. I was twelve at the time."

"My father was married and his wife left him because she resented me. It was then that my father began to sexually molest me. My father couldn't handle me and sent me back to my mother in Eureka. At eighteen, I got hooked on heroin and left home."

"I began to sleep around and got pregnant three times."

"When I got pregnant, I never took drugs because I didn't want the babies to be affected by my drug habit. I put the babies up for adoption because I wanted them to have a mother and a father. I stopped taking heroin and then got addicted to alcohol, but I have been clean and sober for eight years.

"At one time I had a common-law husband who physically abused me and at one time tried to kill me. I left him and ended up homeless. I bought a used van and acquired two dogs, Mooch and Jelly Bean, for protection and companionship. Mooch looks out for Jelly Bean and makes sure to clean her ears and spend time playing with her. I've trained them to treat children and the elderly gently."

One day I found Elizabeth crying and asked, "What is it, Elizabeth?"

Sobbing, she told me that they had taken Mooch and put him in the pound. A lady said that Mooch had attacked her dog. "Mooch would never do that. It was the Lady's dog that attacked Mooch. I'm having a hearing tomorrow at the courthouse."

"Elizabeth, I will go with you and vouch for Mooch"

The next day I met Elizabeth and we went into the courtroom prepared to convince the judge that Mooch was not guilty.

I explained to the judge that Elizabeth was homeless and Mooch protected her and was a source of companionship for her. He was like her child. I went on to say, "Your Honor, I observe Mooch at Plowshares every day and he has never been aggressive and is a very gentle dog."

The judge returned Mooch to Elizabeth. From that day forward, Elizabeth would thank me and tell anyone she met, "Sister Jane got Mooch back for me." She would always add, "I love her."

"I just want to go home," she said one day amid tears.

I asked, "Where is home?"

She responded, "Eureka, where I have lived most of my life. However, I can't leave Ukiah until after my hearing for two parking violations."

"I'll miss you when you're gone!"

"There will be a room awaiting me when I go to Eureka. My uncle who lives in Eureka is arranging to move me into an apartment that has two bedrooms and one and a half bathrooms."

The day arrived, and Elizabeth set out for Eureka.

She called me the next day from Willits, which is twenty miles north of Ukiah. Her van had broken down and she had only two dollars and thirty-eight cents to her name. She called the Mormon Church and two representatives came to her and gave her one hundred thirty dollars. All of the motels were full so she had to stay in her van. She found out that she could rent a van for six hundred dollars a month, and intended to rent a van the following Monday when she received her check. I told her to keep me posted. She assured me that she would call me from Eureka.

Elizabeth called me to say that she had sold her van for two hundred dollars and with her monthly check bought a used car. Her uncle in Eureka came down and got her belongings to be stored in Eureka. He was also looking to put her up in an apartment. She would leave for Eureka on Sunday.

She later called me to say that she arrived safely. Elizabeth is beginning a new life and is elated having a place of her own.

13

I Lost It All

Of all of the guests that I interviewed, Don was the only one who had a normal home life growing up.

He shared with me that he had joined the army when he was eighteen, which was a mistake.

"Sister, I started drinking when I was in the army and got out of the army three years later. I got a well paying job. I met a woman, fell in love and married her. We had two beautiful girls, but my drinking got to a point that my wife left me and took the girls. Employers don't appreciate it when you miss one or two days a week of work. As a result, I lost my job. Soon after, I lost my apartment and ended up living in my car. It wasn't long after that my car was repossessed because I failed to make the car payments.

I ended up on the streets and lived there for twelve years until I got sick and went to Ford Street Rehab Center. They got me to a doctor and I was on medication for two weeks. I never drank during that time."

"While I was at Ford Street, I met Buddy Eller who talked me into going to AA meetings. As a result, I gave up drinking. I now have an apartment, a car and receive disability checks. I have been sober for seventeen years."

"I come to Plowshares to hang out with my old drinking buddies and hope I can influence them to stop drinking. I tell them that their life would be so much better."

One day I asked Don, "Do you have any family?"

"No, Sister."

I gave Don a hug and said,"I'll be your sister."

There was a man standing next to Don who piped in, "Sister, will you be my sister too?"

I gave him a hug and said, "I'll be your sister."

Don loves to greet me with, "Hi, Sis!"

PART III

What Plowshares Means to Me

○ ○
Mary Buckley, our Executive Director, took time out of her busy schedule to interview our guests. She asked them the simple question, "What does Plowshares mean to you?"

These are their stories in their own words and only slightly edited for length.

14

We Would Get Really Frustrated

We came to Plowshares to eat. We would go there just starving, so hungry, like, "Oh, my God, it's almost lunchtime! It's almost lunchtime!" The kids just loved it. Everybody was so nice and helped us so much. They were really sweet and kind to us.

Plowshares was so helpful. They helped us with suggestions of what to do, and who could help us. And having showers and laundry—that was the biggest lifesaver of all! We were camping, horribly grungy and dirty, with no clean clothes to wear and living pretty much out of our car.

We came in just overwhelmed with the situation, really burned out on having no food, no money, no job, nothing. Plowshares was like, "Oh here, you can do laundry, and take showers, and have lunch, If you need to see a doctor, let us know." And being able to use their address was really important, because when you want to get established most places want something stating you have a residence. And being able to use the phone was so much help, because it's quite hard to drive around town all day.

When the baby was sick with a slight ear infection, I was starting to get worried. But the doctor at Plowshares looked at him and reassured us that he was OK. We just needed the security of knowing that when we didn't have any money. Sometimes we would joke about it—five or ten cents to our name! But we always knew that we had at least one meal a day, which helped us a lot. Everybody was really, really kind.

We both had jobs within a week or so after we got here. But not having a home was hard. We would get really, really frustrated. My husband and I just wanted to scream sometimes and say, "We just want to go to sleep in our bed and go home!" But there wasn't a home to go to. There were so many times I would sit and cry.

But we saved up all our money, and did it. We survived through it. Now we have a two-bedroom apartment. We have jobs, and we're doing really well. It's awesome. We have a whole new life up here, starting from scratch, with only thirty dollars to our name. But we got a lot of help from Plowshares.

15

Look at Yourself in the Mirror

I met this guy, and for the longest time it was an abusive relationship. I was beaten, threatened, abused. I was totally petrified—I got cuts, scratches, bruises, and my face was badly bruised and bleeding!

I got picked up for not having a place to live, and I was doing community service. I wound up here at Plowshares.

Plowshares helped, by being here to talk to me, and listening to me, and giving me the courage that I can do it, if I just set my mind to it. I came here crying, being beaten, and you guys got me to the clinic to get fixed up and helped and patched up. Rhonda (staff member) and you guys listened to me and supported me. Rhonda did a hundred percent; she listened to me, she never downed me, and she tried to help me in every way.

One day Rhonda took me in the bathroom and said, "Look in the mirror—see what we see!" It was hard. But I did look, and there is something under there. There is something under that face that said, "You can do better If it wasn't for that, I don't think I could ever have made it. But I had a lot of people telling me, "You can do it if you want." All my life I was told that I was never meant to be anything, you know? I found out otherwise, now, that I can. I know I can. I just got a lot of support here. I came up here for that reason.

My old man who is my new husband tells me daily that I can do better.

I donate my time at Plowshares because it's worth it. If there's another person out there that could just be saved, reach your hands out and help them. That's what it took for me. I've got a wonderful man and a lot of friends that are there to support me and help.

16

Without Plowshares

I've been coming to Plowshares for quite a while now. I'm usually here Monday through Friday. They've got really good food, and the people that work here have a really pleasant attitude; they'll help in anyway they can. I have done laundry here, which has helped me out a lot. I've gotten dog food and miscellaneous things. Some of the saff have helped me fill out applications for college and apartments and everything.

People I don't know come up to me, and I tell them, "Plowshares is real good, because I come here to eat, and they serve good food." I know a lot of people who come here and are homeless or have disabilities or whatever—but to be around other people and be able to talk with them, just to ask them, "How's it going?" and "Have a nice day" makes a big difference to other people. I enjoy it. It helps my day go better.

I'm the type of person who likes to help people in any way I can. Just saying, "Hi, how's it going?" helps another person. That's fantastic. It's an enjoyable place to be. I just love it.

I was really heavy into drugs and ended up homeless a couple of times. At one point, I almost died, and I wanted to change my life because of it. I want to do better and set goals for myself. Coming here, talking to people has helped me, because they give me support and backbone help. That's what's really doing it for me. Plowshares has helped me; they give me direction, help me get on my feet on the right path, and try to help me get going on things that will change my life. I don't know what I would do without Plowshares.

17

How Did You Stop Doing Drugs?

For me, the main thing was I got rid of my partner. I used to do crack. It was really bad. Then I started coming to Plowshares. It took me about a week, and then I thought, you know what? These are people just like me that go there. If I can change my life and start down the right path, somebody else can hear me talk about it and help them to change, because if you listen to other people talk, you can always pick something up. You can learn.

After I got rid of my partner, I set my mind to what I wanted in the future, and I started working towards it. This is where I meet people, this is where I talk to a lot of people, and it helps me to get on the right path to do the things I've done. Once in a while I volunteer here at Plowshares, because they have given me so much, and I love this place. I wouldn't know what to do, or where I'd be without Plowshares.

I'm in the process of trying to find a place to live. I've got several leads and applications out. I'll still come to Plowshares since I can get my hair cut here and get a meal because the food is so good.

A lot of people who come here have not eaten all day. I guess some have drug and alcohol problems … But still they're people. I talk to whoever comes to Plowshares. I offer to help them with any paper work they need help with. I try to give back what I have received.

I started to see the doctor that comes here once a week. I am trying to take care of myself which I never did before.

They have great people that work here, that donate their time and try to help in anyway they can. It's fantastic. I love it here. To me this is like my second home. Since I've been coming here I've been clean and sober. People that know me can see the difference in me. Most of the clothes that I have gotten since I got out of jail I've gotten at Plowshares. When I got out of jail I had just the clothes on my back.

I tell people, this is like home. Good food, even the people that come here and volunteer their time to serve are sweet people. If people could come and see what Plowshares does for people, I don't think they would believe all the stuff you guys do in helping out people. You guys are fantastic.

18

I Will Go to Plowshares

I first became homeless a year ago due to an eviction. I was homeless with my two boys and husband. We moved to the campgrounds and would go to Plowshares for showers and meals when we couldn't afford to buy food. We would wash our clothes at Plowshares.

We moved closer to town and bought a camp-trailer and moved into it. Things became really hard for us. In March of this year, I decided to take my boys and go to Project Sanctuary. I was in an abusive relationship.

Things became hard for us when we were homeless. My husband chose not to work. I was bringing in all the income. I was doing all the childcare. I was the one to see that everyone was clean.

It became too much for me to have the homelessness and the other issues. That's when I chose to go to Project Sanctuary, where they helped me get through the abuse issues. I was there two months with my boys. We have grown tremendously in those two months. The boys continue to do well in school.

I work for the school district and I'm now second on the eligibility list for permanent hire. This is a job that I have been doing off and on for three years. I had a permanent position, and then the funding was cut out for that, so I've been on the substitute list, to get my foot in the door for permanent hire. That's run out now.

Both the boys and I are in family counseling and individual therapy. We go to church every Sunday, which has been very helpful for us. The boys are going to be baptized in the summer at the Calvary Baptist Church. We have game night every Sunday night, and the boys and I do it together.

Things have moved in so many different directions since I decided to leave my abusive situation. The boys will be ten and eight in July. They're perfect attendees in school; they are the only children in their classes that got awards for consistently bringing their homework in every day. My oldest son has more accomplishments under his belt than most adults I know. He is a peer-mediation counselor for this year; he was awarded for that. He was tested to be a member of the GATE (Gifted and Talented Education) program. My younger son is right behind him. I'm proud that they have been able to overcome the bad choices that their parents have made in their lives. We're a happy little threesome. the three of us, and we're going to make it. We are going to edge along. We're now in transitional housing through Project Sanctuary. We have our own place to sleep at night. But I still like to come to Plowshares and have lunch and check for my mail. It's an important part of my life now. The people here are great! I would do anything to give back to this nonprofit organization what they have given me.

I'm happy that I knew enough to say, "I know where we'll go! We'll go to Plowshares. They'll help us."

19

I was skeptical

At first I was skeptical about coming here, because I felt it would be demeaning. Feeling the poverty and feeling the shame is a cold way for me to go, because I've done it most of my life. But dealing with it now is different. Because in my life I have been down but I don't feel that way anymore. This is a blessing in itself. It's like you're treated with respect, and for me that's important. I've done time most of my life, and I've never seen this respect, because of the position I have been in.

I met this lady, and it's like I've got a different attitude, and it's because of her. She's got three kids and a place to stay. She's treated with respect because she treats me with respect. When we come here we don't have to feel funny. I use to feel funny because I've always been in soup kitchens and it's just different.

I stayed in a shelter in Santa Rosa, We had to be out by ten, in by three, that sort of thing. I finally got my own place. Coming here is like the feeling that I get is, you get a good meal. You get treated with respect. I mean, when you walk up you don't have to feel that you're poor. That's a strong feeling for me because I have been poor most of my life. To walk in here and eat and walk out and you're still treated with the same respect, that's important to me. Very important!

20

Conclusion

It is evident from these stories that Plowshares offers more than a hot meal, a place to shower and wash your clothes. It is a place where people are treated with dignity and respect. The staff and volunteers extend a warm welcome and are there to listen and offer advice. For many this proved to be a step toward changing their life. What a wonderful world this would be if all people followed the example of the staff and volunteers at Plowshares. The Kingdom of Heaven would be realized on earth.

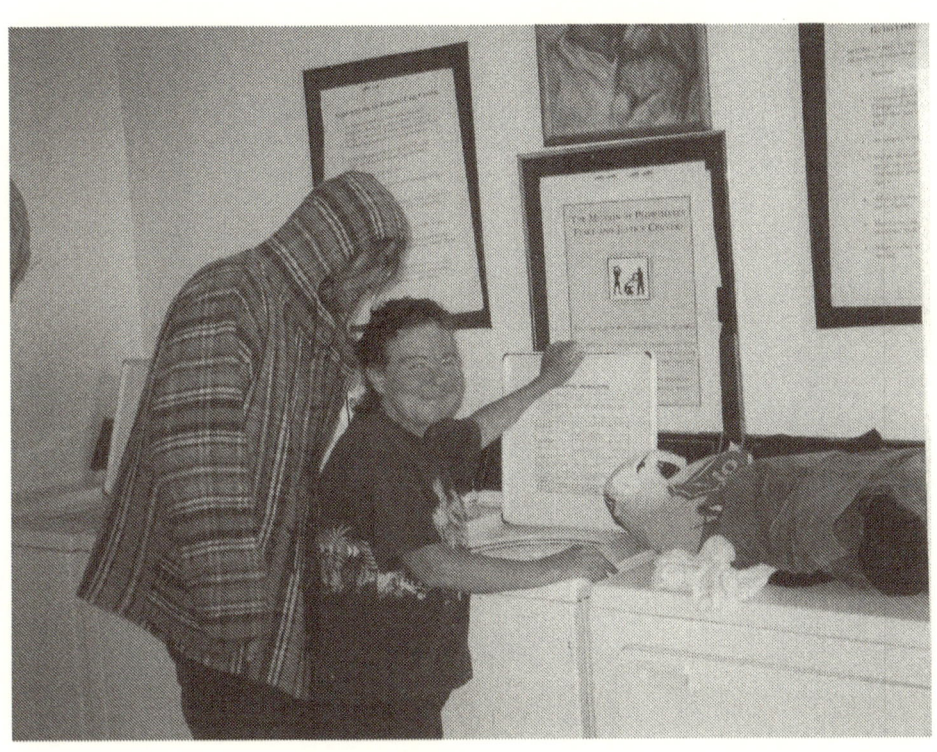

First guest to shower

Ground Breaking for Care Center 10/92

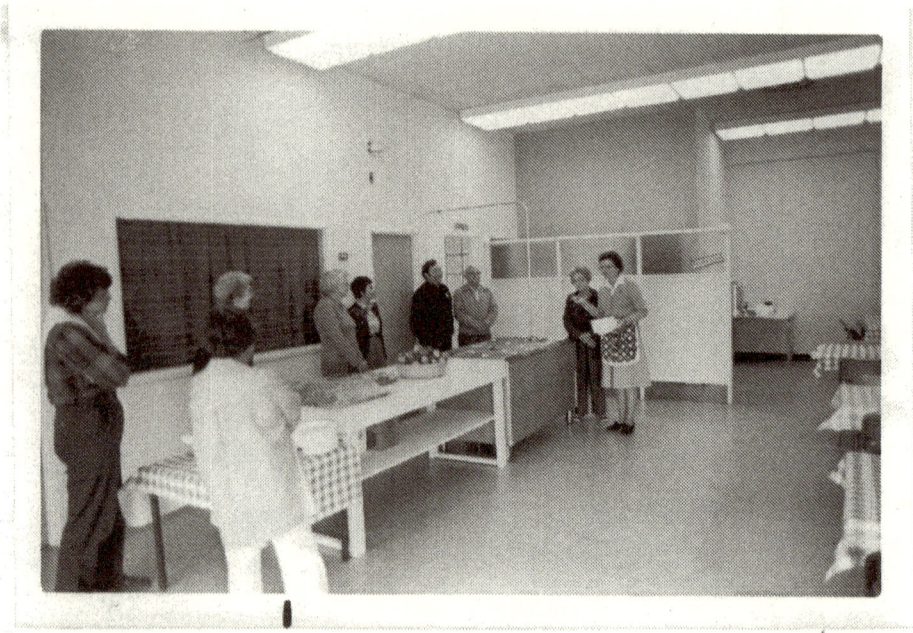

Ready to serve our first meal 11/83

Mary Buckley and Allyne Brown

Sisters Thelma and Jane

Construction of Care center

Sr. Jane Robet Clark Diane Anastasio

Roy Framke, Bev Metcalf, Mary Buckley,
Myrna Terry   Rhonda De Los Santos
Kerri Richardson

978-0-595-45047-3
0-595-45047-4